That Deaf Kid: The Ultimate Guide for Parents of Deaf and Hard of Hearing Children

Mark Drolsbaugh

Published by Handwave Publications, 2022.

While every precaution has been taken in the preparation of this book, the publisher assumes no responsibility for errors or omissions, or for damages resulting from the use of the information contained herein.

THAT DEAF KID: THE ULTIMATE GUIDE FOR PARENTS OF DEAF AND HARD OF HEARING CHILDREN

First edition. February 8, 2022.

ISBN: 979-8201901134

Written by Mark Drolsbaugh.

Table of Contents

To That Deaf Kid. Each and every one of you.

Introduction

That Deaf Kid: The Ultimate Guide for Parents of Deaf and Hard of Hearing Children is a compilation of presentation material based on the book *Madness in the Mainstream.*

There were requests to do presentations all over the United States and Canada after *Madness in the Mainstream* was released. I had a lot of fun with that.

Later, a colleague pointed out that the presentation was as strong, if not stronger, than the actual book. I was flattered, but the realization hit me: If you missed the presentation, then *train gone.*

The presentation is now in print. Problem solved.

In my first book, *Deaf Again,* I advocated on behalf of myself as a deaf person. In *Madness in the Mainstream,* I advocated on behalf of my deaf son. I also have a daughter who later followed the same path. Everything I've written applies to her, too.

When you become a parent, you find a gear you didn't know you had. I found myself writing things that rocked the boat in a way I'd never done before. I want other parents to have this information. A lot of it is kept from them in the early going when they raise deaf and hard of hearing children.

Just like *Madness in the Mainstream,* you'll find a healthy balance of entertaining anecdotes, groundbreaking research, and some *oh my god I can't believe he said that.* You'll laugh, and you'll learn. You'll see the behind-the-scenes impact mainstreaming has on deaf and hard of hearing students. You'll see how these issues can fly under the radar.

More important, you'll see what can be done about it.

Enjoy the madness.

Out of the Frying Pan

I remember what it was like to attend public school in the early 1970s. I was an elementary school student with a progressive sensorineural hearing loss. It was barely noticeable in kindergarten, but I remember becoming increasingly frustrated in first grade.

I also remember there was a special education teacher for those of us who needed extra attention.

Our special education teacher was a film projector.

That's right. If you had any kind of special needs, you could find yourself in a back room with Mr. Projector.

Of course, this was not acceptable. The Education for All Handicapped Children Act, also known as Public Law 94-142, was enacted in 1975. It would later be revised and renamed as the Individuals with Disabilities Education Act (IDEA).

IDEA meant well. It guarantees a free appropriate public education for students with disabilities. A back room with a film projector is obviously not an appropriate education. Thanks to IDEA, many students were taken out of the back room and placed in regular classrooms.

This was a step in the right direction. But if there was one flaw with IDEA, especially when it comes to deaf and hard of hearing children, it was an oversight with LRE.

And what does LRE mean?

Legislators Ruined Everything.

At least they did for the deaf kids, even if it wasn't intentional.

We're talking about *least restrictive environment,* which was meant to open doors for all students with disabilities.

Here's the problem: The general education setting is considered ideal, while a classroom with other people you can actually relate to is considered restrictive.

In other words, *where are the other deaf kids? Peers and role models, you know?*

I wouldn't want to be the only boy in an all-girls school. I wouldn't want to be the only Black child in an all-white school. I wouldn't want to be the only Jewish kid in an all-Catholic school. You get my drift. Being *The Only One* can be uncomfortable. And yet this is what least restrictive environment strives for if you're a deaf child.

If you can fit in with the hearing kids, congratulations! You're practically normal!

Least restrictive environment is supposed to focus on *program* more than *place.* Yet somehow, its interpretation can put deaf kids in the wrong place. A deaf kid in the front row of a large classroom of hearing kids can feel just as isolated as the deaf kid in the back room with Mr. Projector.

The Mona Lisa of All IEPs

During my first year as a guidance counselor at a school for the deaf, my supervisor wanted me to learn how to write an Individualized Education Program. Seeing how I was the new kid on the block, he gave me one of the easiest IEP assignments a counselor could ask for.

I had to write a report on Jeffrey, one of our brightest students. I knew right away this was going to be a piece of cake.

Jeffrey was a brilliant student. Straight A's. He was immensely popular amongst his peers and had a fantastic sense of humor. There were no significant issues of concern as far as I could tell. In fact, this kid's reading and writing skills were way off the charts compared to most deaf students his age.

There's a reason for that. Jeffrey comes from a family that has communicated with him in sign language from birth. He had zero delays in language acquisition.

A disclaimer to all parents reading this: Not every deaf or hard of hearing person out there knows or uses sign language. There are multiple ways a deaf or hard of hearing student can learn, and we'll address that in a later chapter. What I'm saying here is that language acquisition at an early age is the number one key to success. The brain does not care how language is acquired. It could be through sign language, speaking, or communicating in Morse code via armpit farts. Again, the brain doesn't care. It just wants language. Craves it. Language is brain food. Sign language just happens to be the most easily accessible means at the earliest possible age. Jeffrey was living proof of this.

I sat down and typed up the Easiest IEP in the World. It was a classic. It was the Mona Lisa of All IEPs. I printed out a draft and handed it over to my supervisor for review. Then I moseyed back to my office, confident that I had knocked this assignment out of the park.

Five minutes later, there was a knock on my door.

"Uh, Mark?"

It was my supervisor.

"Hi, Steve," I replied. "How was the report?"

"That's why I'm here," Steve sighed.

"Hell of a student, isn't he?" I grinned, completely oblivious to the reality of the situation.

"Uh, yeah." Steve scratched his head. "About that."

Uh-oh.

"It's a good report," Steve continued. "But that's the problem. It's *too good.*"

"Say what?" I was as clueless as ever.

"What you said was great. Completely accurate. But if we use this, the LEA is going to pull Jeffrey out of here and send him back to his home school district."

"What the actual...?"

"Yeah. That's how it works. If he shows too much progress, they'll want him back."

"But he belongs here!"

"You and I both know that," Steve nodded. "But the school district has their own set of rules."

"That's warped, Steve."

"It is. So here's what I need you to do. Look, you did a great job highlighting Jeffrey's strengths. Now I need you to add his *weaknesses.*"

"The kid doesn't have any."

"Okay, his *needs.* He *needs* hearing aids and consistent audiological support. He *needs* speech therapy. He *needs* counseling support because sometimes he has anger issues."

"Okay, got it," I nodded, finally understanding how this worked.

I reopened the file and added some finishing touches to what used to be the Mona Lisa.

A mustache. Bushy eyebrows. A piece of snot.

I handed in a revised draft of my defiled Mona Lisa.

"This is perfect," said Steve.

Just so you know: Jeffrey's IEP meeting went great. He was able to remain in our school and graduated a few years later. Today, he's a college graduate and gainfully employed.

8

Ambushed at the IEP Meeting

Twelve years after Jeffrey's IEP, I found myself on the opposite side of the table. My own son, Darren, was diagnosed with a progressive sensorineural hearing loss.

Disclaimer: There are people who can't stand the term "hearing loss." I get it. It has a negative connotation. Ask them to explain another term, Deaf Gain, and you'll have your mind opened to an entirely new perspective. But for my son and I (and later my daughter, Lacey), we do indeed have a hearing loss. We're late-deafened. We used to be able to hear, and we lost that. No amount of semantics can change that fact. While we absolutely did gain other things, that would be later. Much later.

After all of those years working in the school system with deaf kids, you'd think I was the Master of All IEPs. Nope. If you thought IEPs were overwhelming for teachers, it's a lot harder for parents. At Darren's first IEP meeting, I was like a deer in the headlights.

On that fateful day, I sat in the lobby outside of the principal's office for what felt like an eternity. I was accompanied by my wife, Melanie.

"You think they'll be receptive to what we want?" I asked.

"They have to," Melanie replied. "It's the law."

"I don't know. I have a bad feeling about this."

Finally, a secretary invited us in. She opened the door and...

What the hell? The room was packed to capacity.

It was standing room only. There was a guy outside shouting *"Tickets! Who needs tickets? Get your tickets to the Drolsbaugh IEP! It's gonna be a bar fight! Get your tickets here!"*

A huge conference table was surrounded by elementary school staff, administrators, and a couple of representatives from the school district.

Another disclaimer: The teachers and administrative staff at Darren's elementary school (and later, middle school) were always good to us. It's just that sometimes politics from the top trickles downhill and makes things more difficult than they have to be.

After the customary introductions, the battle was on. It was clear from the start that one of the reps from the school district was running the show.

"...and in order to maintain Darren's academic progress, it's highly recommended that he gets evaluated for a cochlear implant."

Excuse me?

Nothing personal against the cochlear implant, but if we're getting recommendations from the school district, I want *everything* on the table. Offer us hearing aids, an FM system, an ASL interpreter, a cochlear implant, CART, a notetaker, a deaf program, whatever else is available, and let us sort it out. But no, this rep from the school district offered *only* the cochlear implant.

"No," said Melanie. "We want to start with an ASL interpreter."

The school district rep shifted uncomfortably in her seat.

"We really recommend starting with the cochlear implant. Darren would be a great candidate for it."

Melanie and I looked at each other in disbelief. That's when the realization struck.

What if we were hearing parents who knew nothing about sign language and the deaf community? We'd still be traumatized from the initial diagnosis and Darren would be on his way to Children's Hospital of Philadelphia for cochlear implant surgery as soon as possible. We wouldn't know what else to do. We wouldn't know who else to trust.

"No," I repeated. "We come from a deaf family. We respect the progress medical technology has made, but we also know that it's not a prerequisite for success. Access to information is. ASL offers that and Darren gets a lot of it at home. Might as well continue with it at school. So we'd like to go with an ASL interpreter."

The school district rep squirmed in her seat as she tried her best to maintain her composure.

"How about this," she offered. "Go get evaluated for a cochlear implant first, and then get an interpreter if that doesn't work out."

Melanie and I shook our heads in disagreement.

"It takes time to get a cochlear implant," Melanie emphasized. "We don't want to waste any more time. Darren is falling behind right now."

"But wait…" the school district rep protested.

"That's the problem," Melanie interrupted. "You're asking us to wait. If we did what you're suggesting, first we would have to make an appointment with a doctor. We'd probably have to wait a few weeks to see a specialist. Then Darren would need to go through some tests to decide whether or not he'd benefit from a cochlear implant. Assuming they say yes, then we would have to schedule surgery at a later date. More waiting. After that, we'd have to wait a month before the implant could be activated. I'm sure you're aware that merely activating the implant won't turn him into a hearing person. The next step would be mapping and subsequent training sessions to get him acclimated to the implant. You're asking us to wait that long before he *might* hear well enough to learn in class? That's asking a lot."

"But it might be worth it," the school district rep insisted. "We need to find out."

"We need to have Darren learning *now*," Melanie responded. "Darren already knows ASL. Put an ASL interpreter in class and he will *instantaneously* have full access. He can continue to learn, right now, without missing a beat. We don't want him missing information any longer than he already has."

Finally, the school district rep relented. We got the interpreter. Melanie and I needed a stiff drink.

Little did we know that fifteen years later, we'd have more IEP meetings with our late-deafened daughter, Lacey. That thing I said earlier about politics from the top trickling downhill? It didn't apply anymore. During Lacey's initial IEP meeting, we had the luxury of knowing that the vice president of the school board was an experienced teacher of the deaf. He gets it. Ditto for Lacey's itinerant teacher. This time around, everyone was on our side. Having this kind of support really made things easier for Melanie and me. But for Lacey? It was still tough. While she got a ton of support from professionals who fully understood her needs, the mainstream environment itself was still a challenge. There are three thousand students at Lacey's high school. It's unrealistic to expect such a large number of people who are not deaf to fully understand the perspective of a deaf person.

A Tale of Two Deaf Schools

The IEP fiasco with my son struck me hard. It was clear from the get-go that the focus was entirely on the Auditory-Verbal Therapy approach first. The school district's game plan leaned heavily toward the cochlear implant. If that didn't work, there were always hearing aids, FM systems, and Communication Access Realtime Translation (CART). While you're at it, throw some speech therapy in there.

I'm not saying any of those options are wrong. They work for some. My problem is with the *order* in which they were presented. And they didn't even put everything on the table. They offer one Auditory-Verbal option at a time, in order, until everything has been checked off. If none of that works, then, and only then, will deaf-friendly options such as sign language or a deaf program be offered.

Newsflash: It doesn't have to be that way. You can use hearing aids or cochlear implants AND use sign language.

This was my beef at the IEP. Yeah, beef. As in *where's the beef?* Remember that old Wendy's commercial? I wanted to see the beef. And the fries. A frosty. I want the whole menu. Don't offer me one option at a time until we find something agreeable. Does Wendy's show you one burger and then move on to the fries only if you don't want the burger? No. They show you the whole freaking menu! Why can't an IEP meeting be the same? It can, and should be.

So when Melanie and I left that IEP meeting, we realized that no one was on the same page. More specifically, we realized that our interpretation of *Deaf School* and the school district's interpretation of *Deaf School* were two entirely different things.

Our interpretation: A hearing school is a place where kids listen, mostly with their ears, and learn. A deaf school is a place where kids listen, mostly with their eyes, and learn. Both are quality educational options, on equal footing, offering equal opportunities to succeed based on their respective students' strengths.

The school district's interpretation: A hearing school is *the ideal.* It is superior to the deaf school and is in fact legally recognized as the least restrictive environment. A deaf school is a last resort. It should only be considered if all else has failed.

And here's the result of this discrepancy: More often than not, deaf and hard of hearing children are steered toward mainstream schools first.

The message delivered to deaf and hard of hearing children?

You have to function as a hearing person.

This is where everything starts to go wrong.

Reality Check

Back when I was in grade school, slowly going deaf, there was a common refrain from my teachers:

He's doing fine! He's just like any normal hearing person!

Not so fast. There's a big difference between perception and reality.

I was a classic introvert all the way through my K-12 years. I often looked studious, as if I knew what I was doing. I didn't. I thought *I was supposed to look like I knew what I was doing.* That I was supposed to fit in. So I did my best to look the part.

But the reality? I spent most of my class time daydreaming. What else was there to do if I didn't understand anything the teachers said?

I also engaged in social bluffing. We'll go deeper into that later. My point, for now, is that I often looked like a kid who had it together. In reality, my mind was somewhere on another planet.

Decades later, a similar discord between perception and reality occurred during a disagreement with my wife. She comes from a family where everyone is handy. She expects me to be the same.

Not going to happen.

There are people in her family who can literally build houses from scratch. Her dad used to buy junkyard cars and completely rebuild them. He'd spiff them up so good, they'd win awards at car shows. Meanwhile, I struggle to change a light bulb.

Over time, I've improved. I can fix a toilet. I've repaired a lawn mower. *Yay.* But for whatever reason, Melanie thinks I'm Bob Vila. She often asks me to do fix-it projects around the house without noticing that most of the time, I'm in over my head.

One project she asked me to do was to install a coat rack in our closet. It seemed simple enough. Melanie encouraged me along the lines of *even you can do this.*

So I installed the coat rack. The most complicated part (for me, at least) was drilling four holes in the wall.

The first three holes were no problem. *I got this,* I thought to myself. So of course, that last hole was a challenge. It was tough to drill and I really had to push through to get it done. But I did get it done. I beamed in pride at my handiwork.

A short time later, I went downstairs to clean the litter box.

What the hell?

The litter box was downright *soaked.*

"Mel! Did you give Lucky some of my beer? That cat peed in the litter box like there's no tomorrow."

"Don't be silly," Melanie replied. "What happ- *oh my god.*" She and I looked up at the ceiling.

There was a leak. Coming right from where I drilled those holes a while ago.

"Dude," said my brother-in-law, who came over to fix the problem. "If you're drilling a hole in the wall and you hit something... for chrissakes, *stop.*"

But I digress. Melanie still thinks I'm Bob Vila when I'm actually Al Bundy. I tried to tell her as much. She wouldn't have it. We went back and forth for a while until the argument took an unexpected turn.

"Oh, stop it," she said. "You exaggerate. You can easily do this stuff."

"Come on, Mel," I implored. "I suck at this. Your mind is so full of who you want me to be, you don't see who I really am."

We froze. Instant mind-meld.

"Wow. You ought to write that down."

"I will," I replied, shaking my head in full agreement.

I put that quote on paper. Modified it a little. And now we have the mainstream experience in a nutshell:

Their minds are so full of who they want us to be, they don't see who we really are.

A Tale of Two Case Studies

In order to fully to assess a situation, it helps to have a frame of reference. A lot of deaf and hard of hearing children, as well as their parents, don't have this frame of reference.

Here's an interesting tidbit: When I first offered my deaf son an opportunity to go to a deaf school, he said no. It wasn't until he interacted with deaf peers and deaf teachers at a summer camp when he said he would like to give it a try.

Finally, at the age of fourteen, Darren had a frame of reference that many of us don't have. He walked a mile in two worlds. He figured it out.

If you read Deaf Again, *you'll see that I didn't figure this stuff out until I was twenty-three. Darren is way ahead of me in the wisdom department.*

Let's start with his mainstreaming experience. After that IEP from hell, he did great in school. He had hearing aids, an ASL interpreter, speech therapy, and the support of an itinerant teacher. His grades were consistently good.

For all intents and purposes, the supplementary aids and services did their job. Darren succeeded in what was considered the least restrictive environment of his local hearing school.

But after Darren went to a deaf school, he was able to describe the difference between the two educational settings. He did so in great detail. From his perspective, here's the scoop:

Mainstream school: Most of the information came from teachers via an ASL interpreter. Due to the slight time delay that comes with spoken English being translated into ASL, there were times when Darren raised his hand to answer a question, only to find that a classmate had already answered it. Meanwhile, there was not much of the incidental learning that comes from interaction with peers. And although he played on the baseball team, most of the interaction was on the field. After the game, it was always "Good game, see you later." He was rarely invited to social events. When he was, he was often a wallflower.

Deaf School: Darren had direct, real-time communication with his teachers and classmates. He was able to participate in classroom conversation. This included content-related discussion as well as off-the-cuff topics and jokes. Conversation didn't end there. There were cafeteria conversations, hallway conversations, and conversation in the dorm. Opportunities for incidental learning via peer interaction was plentiful. In sports, he played both football and baseball. Conversation was everywhere, not just on the field. Darren participated in locker room conversation, pre-game warmup conversation, bench and dugout conversation, and conversations on the bus to and from games. There was no "Good game, see you later." Instead, it was "Good game. Want to hang out tonight?" As for social gatherings, he was a regular participant.

Which environment do you think is least restrictive?

The contrast between the two settings is like night and day. Of course, we're only talking about one person. Some people have said, "interesting perspective, but that's just *your* kid. What happened to him doesn't necessarily apply to everyone else."

Point taken. We need more research.

And we have it!

Let's take a look at Dr. Mindy Hopper's dissertation titled *Positioned as Bystanders: Deaf Students' Experiences and Perceptions of Informal Learning Phenomena.*

Among the research Dr. Hopper compiled was data from a freewriting experiment involving a mainstreamed deaf student and a hearing student. She had the deaf student and the hearing student, each from the same school, writing journal entries about their daily experiences.

As soon as these two students arrived at school, they were to document everything they saw, heard, and learned on the bus. They did the same thing, I believe, after lunch in the cafeteria.

I don't have access to those students' journals so I can't share specific content. I only have the general outcome of the study, which I will share soon. But speaking as a former mainstreamed student and as a parent of a mainstreamed student, I can give you a good idea of what it's like for any mainstreamed deaf student on a school bus. Here's how it can go down:

A deaf student gets on the bus. She notices the bus driver seems a bit cranky. She shrugs and moves on to her seat. She notices the girl who normally sits next to her is absent. Across the row, she notices a boy with brand new basketball shoes. Nice. She says hello to a classmate, and notices that classmate brought earmuffs with her. Interesting.

Meanwhile, a hearing student gets on the same bus. She notices the cranky driver and lowers her head. She feels bad because she heard the driver is going through a nasty divorce. She sits down in her seat and says to the student next to her, "Uh-oh. Laura's absent. I heard she got that nasty stomach virus that's going around." The other student replies, "Yeah. It's a norovirus. It'll make you puke your guts out." Up until that point, the hearing student had never heard the word *norovirus*. Just like that, she adds another word to her vocabulary bank.

Then she sees Mike, the kid with the new basketball shoes. "I heard you had a good game last night, Mike," she says. Another student jumps into the conversation. "Are you kidding me?" she marvels. "Mike hit the game-winning shot with two seconds left. The place went nuts." The hearing girl smiles and glances over to the girl with the earmuffs. While this is happening, she can hear the weather report on the bus driver's radio. A meteorologist announces that a cold front is on the way, and temperatures will drop thirty degrees by early evening. That girl with the earmuffs is always prepared.

See the difference? This is the kind of thing Dr. Hopper uncovered.

After the allotted time for freewriting was up, Dr. Hopper brought these two students together. She allowed them to look at each other's notes. The reaction, which Dr. Hopper documented, spoke volumes.

"Oh my god," the deaf girl exclaimed, as she read through her hearing classmate's notes. "I had *no idea* I was missing this much."

She had no idea because she had no frame of reference.

She does now.

It's a sobering realization. But again, someone may point out that this is just another solitary deaf kid. That deaf kid and my deaf kid are a ridiculously small sample size.

Point taken.

But wait! There's more!

This presentation material is based on my book, *Madness in the Mainstream.* But that's not the only game in town. You might like to know it was inspired by another book, *Alone in the Mainstream* by Dr. Gina Oliva.

There's another one. It's a real beaut. Check out *Turning the Tide: Making Life Better for Deaf and Hard of Hearing Schoolchildren* by Dr. Gina Oliva and Dr. Linda Risser Lytle. It has a significant sample size of deaf and hard of hearing people shining light on the mainstream experience.

In a nutshell, a lot of us are saying the same thing. No one's listening. No pun intended.

Mainstream Survival Skills

A common refrain that I often heard throughout my mainstream school years was *"He's doing fine! He's just like any normal hearing person!"*

I certainly gave that impression. I put on an Oscar performance where I (almost) fooled everyone, including myself.

When you feel it's your responsibility to fit in, you'll do anything to accomplish that. Including the utilization of what I call Mainstream Survival Skills. I've done it, my kids have done it. We've all done it.

Let's start with the most common mainstream survival skill: The infamous human bobblehead doll.

When someone says something and we don't understand, we quickly go on Bobblehead Standby Alert. For example, I might say "whazzat?" once or twice. But there's no way I'm going to do that a third time. If I don't get it during the first two attempts, I'll go into Bobblehead Mode. I'll keep nodding my head until it gets me out of an uncomfortable situation.

This can backfire, though. If someone's just chattering away, that's fine. Nod your head as much as you want and no one will know the difference. But if someone asks you a question...

"What time is it?"

(Nods)

That obviously doesn't work. You have to develop a feel for it. But again, it's much easier to nod your head than to ask people to repeat things over and over.

When I was in school, I learned to differentiate between a statement and a question. The game plan was to nod at the statements and say "I don't know" to the questions.

I said "I don't know" a lot. It was my preference to look stupid rather than look deaf. My rationale? There are plenty of stupid people. I preferred to blend in with the stupid rather than draw attention to myself as the lone deaf kid.

Of course, this backfires. I'll never forget the day we had a substitute teacher and she asked me a question.

"I don't know," I shrugged.

The class erupted in laughter.

What the hell?

Turns out the teacher asked me what my name was.

"What's your name?"

"I don't know."

That obviously did not go well.

Okay. We've established that nodding or acting stupid is not really a good strategy. It still remains the number one option. Next time you see a deaf kid going "uh-huh, uh-huh," ask that kid to repeat what you just said. It's a sobering reality check.

We have other mainstream survival skills, though. Some of them actually work. One of my favorites is called "last in line at gym." I got away with this one all the time.

Our gym teacher would have us sit in a circle as he explained the rules for a new game or activity. I sat there nodding. No idea what was going on. At all.

"All right, everyone," the gym teacher barked. "Line up! Let's go!"

Everyone got up and ran to form a line. Except me. I took my damn time. Because I was in no hurry to be at the front of that line. I needed time to do some surveillance.

From the back of the line, I'd watch intently as my classmates did whatever it was that we were instructed to do. By the time it was my turn, I'd seen enough and knew the drill. Most of the time, I'd get it right.

It worked. So much, in fact, that my gym teacher often gave glowing reviews of my performance in class.

"What a brave kid," he marveled. "He doesn't miss a beat. He's just like any normal hearing person!"

"Whew," I thought to myself. "Fooled him."

Sometimes I used the "Bluff and Use an Informant" technique. When my history teacher gave a lecture, I was the only student looking at her. My head went left-right, left-right, left-right as she paced the room. If you looked at me, you'd think I was watching a tennis match. Not good. I didn't want it to be obvious that I was working hard to read my teacher's lips.

I looked around at my classmates. My hearing classmates. The ones who weren't even looking at the teacher. Some of them casually glanced around the room as they listened to the lecture. Others diligently took notes. I have no idea how many of them were actually paying attention, but they did look like they were listening intently.

I wanted to look the same.

It reached the point where I didn't even bother looking at the teacher anymore, except for the occasional glance. If another student had a question or comment, I'd briefly glance at that student as well. Then I'd go back to doodling in my notebook. It actually looked like I was taking notes. I was, if you count drawing Mickey Mouse cartoons as notes.

That was the "bluff" part. But the key to pulling off this charade was to have a reliable informant.

Every mainstreamed kid knows who I'm talking about. In every school, there's always that one person you know you can depend on. The nice person who gladly offers help when you ask. An informant. I had at least one in each class.

I'd draw cartoons in my notebook with a serious expression on my face, and the second the bell rang, I'd run up to my informant.

"Yo, Brian! What did Mrs. Wilson say the homework was? Ah, got it. Thanks, pal."

Armed with this intel from my trusted informant, I'd go home and get my homework done.

Uh, not so fast.

Sometimes the homework involved topics or questions that weren't answered in the textbook.

Shit.

I'm an old fart. This happened long before Google. I had to go to this place called a library. I'd walk five miles uphill in the snow to the library, find the information I needed, then walk five miles uphill in the snow back home.

The next day, I'd hand in my homework. Nailed it.

"Great job, Mark!" Mrs. Wilson exclaimed. She would later tell other teachers I was a great kid who... repeat after me... *"is just like any normal hearing person!"*

"Whew," I thought to myself. "Fooled her."

There's more.

Would you believe music class?

That's right. I was required to attend music class. At least for a while. At no point, being the only deaf kid, did I ever stand up for myself and say, *"Hey! I'm deaf! What are you putting me in a choir for?"*

For the life of me, I wish I could go back in time and join that class again. I would *love* to belt a tune at the top of my lungs and shatter every window in the building. Make *them* question the decision to put me in there.

But no, I felt it was my responsibility to fit in. So I studied the lyrics for every song we covered. I lip synched. I put Milli Vanilli to shame.

Oh, it gets worse. I somehow found a way to lip synch in history class, too. We had this thing called Greek Week. Each history class would select a famous Greek play, rehearse for a couple of months, and then put on a big performance during Greek Week.

My tenth grade history teacher had more common sense than my music teacher. She knew I wasn't up for a starring role, so she put me in the Greek chorus. To my relief, this chorus didn't do any actual singing. We were just narrators. All we had to do was mumble a few lines in between scenes.

Of course, I didn't want to use my deaf voice in an auditorium packed with other students and their families. Once again, it was lip synch time. Using a series of index cards, I studied and memorized the lines of the Greek chorus. My eyes would glance downward at the cards, and then sideways at other members of the chorus.

Eventually I got the timing down. I memorized the lines to the point where I didn't need the index cards anymore. By observing everyone else, I had a good sense of when to say what.

Note: "Deaf" does not mean totally deaf. Every deaf person has varying levels of hearing ability. I could hear the cadence of the chorus, even if I had no idea what they were saying. After memorizing the lines, I then knew what they were saying. I was able to keep up.

It reached the point where it looked like I fit in. My lips moved in perfect synchronization with everyone else. But damned if I was going to use my voice.

During our final rehearsal the day before our big performance, our teacher, Mrs. Clark, walked around the stage as we went through our lines. As she strode past the chorus, she stopped momentarily, then kept going.

Whew!

After rehearsal, I grabbed my backpack and headed out the—

"Mark, do you have a minute?" Mrs. Clark asked.

Awww, shit.

I stopped in my tracks. I knew what was coming.

"I couldn't help but notice you were lip synching," she said.

Busted.

"Mark," she continued. "You have a beautiful voice. Stand proud. Use it. I know you can do it."

"Uh, okay?" I squirmed.

I gave it some thought. You know what? What the hell. The next evening, in front of two hundred people, I let loose. Released the Kraken. My beautiful deaf voice reverberated across the auditorium.

Windows cracked. Cockroaches scurried out of the building. Dogs howled. I didn't care.

After the show, Mrs. Clark ran up to me. Tears welled up in her eyes. She gave me a bear hug.

"Mark, I heard you! That was so beautiful! You have a beautiful, loud, clear voice!"

"Um, okay?"

Whew.

But wait! I'm not done yet. We have two more survival skills to cover. The next one is simply "working the room." It's exactly what it sounds like. It's usually implemented in a more informal setting. It could be at a school or family social event.

All you have to do is go up to different people, say "hi, how you doing?" and manage a brief one-on-one conversation. Then get the hell out of there.

The whole point is to manage a superficial conversation, which anyone can do. You can pretty much predict where small talk is going. You know what to look for when lipreading. But if you stick around too long, the conversation might take a deeper, unexpected twist. At which point you'll be totally lost.

Bail out!

In one of my other books, I mentioned meeting a twelve-year-old kid who had nailed this technique. He was the Master of How Do Ya Do. He worked the room like a seasoned politician. All he had to do was kiss a few babies and ask for your vote, and he'd be president by now.

I met this kid during a Family Learning Vacation at the Governor Baxter School for the Deaf in Maine. He shared this method with me in front of a big group of other deaf and hard of hearing kids. It hit me hard when they nodded their heads in acknowledgement that they, too, had done the same thing.

"Isn't that exhausting?" I asked.

"Yeah," the kid confirmed. "Sometimes I sneak out and go to my room to play Nintendo for a while."

That's a lot of work.

I'm not done yet. There's one more. Here's one that I have done several times:

Dominate the conversation.

It's simple. Someone says hello. You take a deep breath and then start talking. And talking. And talking and talking and talking and - keep going!- talking and talking. Don't give the other guy any room to get a word in edgewise. Yap away!

Here's why this works: If I'm talking, and you're not, there's zero chance of me misunderstanding anything you say. Because I'm not allowing you to say anything at all! How brilliant is that?

There you have it. Mainstream Survival Skills. Utilized by deaf and hard of hearing kids of all ages. Because, unless we learn otherwise, we think we have to.

Introjection

Those mainstream survival skills we just covered are absolutely clever. They're also a lot of work. It takes a considerable amount of effort to pull that off.

If you're a politician and you want to BS your way through life, that's a career choice. But we're talking about young kids going to great extremes to provide the illusion that they're doing fine.

That twelve-year-old kid? He was exhausted. And yet he went to great lengths to maintain the charade.

Why?

I'll tell you why.

Introjection.

One of my best learning experiences was a class at the Modern Gestalt Institute. It was taught by Dolly Schulman. I have to give her a shout-out. She understood me more than I understood myself. As her class went on, she patiently and methodologically got me to take a good look at myself. It was a mind-blowing experience.

Dolly got me to understand how this thing called *introjection* can block people from being their genuine selves.

Introjection is basically known as a resistance where we (paraphrasing Erving & Miriam Polster in *Gestalt Therapy Integrated: Contours of Theory & Practice*) "incorporate what the environment provides," "swallow whole impressions of the world," and "give up a sense of free choice in life."

Introjects are a powerful influence that literally program our minds and shape our behavior. Let's take a look at a few examples. Below are some apparently harmless phrases that kids are exposed to on a daily basis:

Finish your plate.

If you don't stop making goofy faces, your face will freeze like that.

Big boys don't cry.

You should... (insert any guilt-inducing objective here).

As I said, apparently harmless. But if you take a closer look, words like these have more power than we ever could have imagined. For example, let's break down *big boys don't cry.*

I guarantee you that at any movie theater in the country, if you observe a man and a woman watching to a movie together, you'll find an interesting contrast in behavior.

If the movie has a strong emotional impact—be it a heart-tugging happy ending or a tear-jerking tragedy—you can bet that the woman has no qualms about crying in full view of everyone.

The guy, on the other hand, is more fun to watch. He'll gulp. His lips will quiver. He'll pretend he's got something stuck in his eye. If you ask him if he's okay, he'll swear nothing's wrong. He'll emit a fake yawn, stretch out his arms, and discreetly brush away a tear rolling down his cheek. He's practically imploding.

It wasn't the movie that wigged him out. You have to go back in time to locate the source of this behavior.

Imagine this man several years ago when he was a little kid. He's playing football in the backyard with some family and friends when all of a sudden, he slips and scrapes his knee. Naturally, he starts crying. And then someone says the magic words: *"Oh, come on, suck it up! Big boys don't cry. Man up."*

That's all it takes. This boy has now been programmed by an introject. He absorbs and internalizes this message. It becomes his reality. And then, twenty years later, you can find him in the movie theater having a spastic fit.

Introjects don't have to be verbal. Kids watch their parents' behavior and internalize just about anything. The age-old curse *"I hope someday you wind up having kids just like you!"* definitely works. Like it or not, most of us emulate our parents in ways that are quite uncanny. Without even realizing it, many kids literally walk, talk, and demonstrate the same idiosyncrasies as their parents.

And now we're ready to bring this discussion back to deaf identity. With the previous examples in mind, let's look at introjects that have a significant impact on deaf kids:

1. Sit up front. Pay attention. Read my lips.

This implies that communication is a one-way street. It suggests that it's the deaf person's responsibility to understand everything.

2. Wear your hearing aids.

We have to be careful with this one. There's nothing wrong with hearing aids (or cochlear implants, for that matter). A lot of deaf people love their hearing aids. It's not the technology itself. It's the *overemphasis* of it. If you push, prod, and implore your deaf kids to wear hearing aids at all times, as if their lives depended on it, you're sending the wrong message.

Let me elaborate with a parallel scenario. I'm a baseball lifer. Love the game. All of my kids have played baseball and softball. It's a beautiful game. We've been to a ton of games and tournaments. Great experience.

But you know what? Every year, we see *That Dad*. The one running up and down the foul lines, waving at his kid, trying to give unsolicited advice. The one undermining the coaches and screaming at the umpires. The one who immediately wants to do a recap of the game with his son during the car ride home. You can see the body language on the poor kid.

Baseball's a great game, but *That Dad* can turn it into a nightmare. If he had any common sense, the conversation during the ride home would be *where should we go for ice cream* instead of *what happened with that error in the fifth inning.*

Don't be *That Dad* in any aspect of your kid's life. Including hearing aids and cochlear implants.

3. *Hearing impaired / can't hear.*

Again, I'm an old fart. But I can remember, as far back as third grade, seeing adults say this right in front of me: *"This is Mark. He's hearing impaired. He can't hear. You have to look at him directly when you speak to him."*

I can tell you without a doubt that the words "impaired" and "can't" ring loudly in our heads. It's worse than tinnitus. When you see *can't... can't... can't...* you internalize it. In many areas of your life.

4. *"He's just like any other normal hearing person" and any other praise for hearing-centric behavior.*

All of those teachers I told you about? Including the one who bear-hugged me after I rocked the auditorium with my loud, clear, deaf voice? They loved me and I loved them. But it needs to be said that they also reinforced my internalized belief that I had to be this *normal hearing person* that they so badly wanted. Which is hard to do when you're deaf.

There's one more introject I have that isn't so much about words, but of a powerful visual impression:

5. *Directives from medical professionals (especially without input from deaf professionals).*

Whenever a child is identified as deaf, the first place a family goes to is the doctor's office. When you're a little kid and you see that grown adult in the white coat, you *know* that person is a highly-revered authority figure. An expert.

He's wearing that white jacket. He must know what he's talking about. And nine times out of ten, he's going to say things that reinforce those introjects we've discussed.

All of the above sends a clear, unmistakable message.

You need to act hearing. It is your responsibility to assimilate.

When we expose deaf and hard of hearing children to all of the above, we're instilling in them a model of deficit thinking. We're telling these kids that deafness is bad. We're telling them they're *impaired.* We're telling them that they need to look, think, and act like hearing people.

Now you know why that twelve-year-old kid worked the room the way that he did.

These introjects can weigh down a deaf person for a lifetime. It's a formidable obstacle to overcome.

Introject Overload

Before we move on from introjects, there's a powerful quote I would like to share with you. It's from zencaroline.blogspot.com. I have no idea who Caroline is. But as far as Gestalt goes, she nailed it. Here's an excerpt:

"...the man who introjects never gets a chance to develop his own personality, because he is so busy holding down the foreign bodies he has swallowed whole. The more introjects he has saddled himself with, the less room there is for him to express or even discover what he himself is."

That is *exactly* what we're dealing with. If you saddle yourself with too many introjects, you lose track of who you are.

Case in point: If you invented a time machine, or if you just borrowed Doc Brown's juiced-up DeLorean that sent Marty McFly back to the future, set the dial on 1984. Look for me. You'll be surprised at what you find.

You'll find me during my senior year in high school. And even though I have an ASL interpreter, you'll still catch me using a lot of those mainstream survival skills. My interpreter couldn't follow me around 24/7 so there were plenty of times when I had to fend for myself. The need for those mainstream survival skills never fully went away.

Now go up to the 1984 me and ask him how he's doing. You know what he's going to say?

"I'm doing great! I'm going to graduate soon. I'm just like any other normal hearing person!"

Yes. In a weird way, I internalized everything around me. I thought I was doing great.

Now hop back in the DeLorean and set it to 1989. Look me up again. You know what the 1989 me is going to say?

"I was an idiot in 1984."

That's right. In 1989 I went to Gallaudet University. It's the world's only university for deaf and hard of hearing students. It was the first time I was in a classroom with other people who were *just like me.*

Oh my god! I'm not the only one!

It gets better. Several of my *teachers* were *just like me.* They were successful deaf role models. Up until then, I didn't really understand that it was common for deaf people to attain that level of success. In fact, prior to attending Gallaudet, I had worked as a stock clerk in a supermarket. I thought that was as good as it gets for a deaf guy. I was mentally prepared to work in that supermarket for forty years.

And then at Gallaudet, I saw all of these deaf professors with Ph.Ds. There were also numerous deaf professionals with all kinds of exciting jobs in Washington D.C. and its surrounding regions.

Hey! Did you know there's a deaf dentist? That blew my mind. I thought that was impossible.

A self-imposed glass ceiling soon shattered.

All of those introjects that latched onto me before? They had formed a shell around me. I had spent many years living in that shell. Completely oblivious of who I really was, completely oblivious of who I could be.

At Gallaudet, that shell cracked. The real me stepped out.

Hey! I'm here. This is me. Wow. Feels great. How ya like me now?

Cochlear Implants

I'm pretty sure that some of you might be thinking *interesting presentation, but it doesn't apply to kids who have cochlear implants.*

I once thought the same thing, too.

Back in the 1990s, I was aghast when I learned about the cochlear implant. I was against it for too many reasons to list here.

But you can't ignore technology. Nothing drove that point home harder than one of my former teachers at Gallaudet, the late Dr. Allen Sussman. It was Dr. Sussman who instilled in me a sense of deaf pride on a level that few others could match. He helped me understand and embrace my deaf identity.

And then one day, I saw him give a keynote address at this huge conference, where he floored me with these words:

"The cochlear implant is here to stay."

He was right.

Over the years, the cochlear implant improved. It kept getting better. That's what technology does. There are plenty of cochlear implant success stories out there, and I can't help noticing them.

Finally, it reached the point where I gave this disclaimer at one of my earlier presentations:

"It's possible that thanks to the cochlear implant, everything I've ever written could become obsolete."

I tossed a copy of *Madness in the Mainstream* over my shoulder for added effect.

"NOOOOOOOOOOOOOO!!!!!" shouted someone a few rows back.

It was the mother of a deaf child with a cochlear implant. She had a few things to say. I gladly granted her the opportunity.

"My child is doing great academically," she explained. "But she has no friends. She can focus on the teacher and follow lessons quite well. Groups are different. Socializing is hard."

Other parents have made similar comments over the years. Many also said something along the lines of "the hospital never told us about sign language and the deaf community." These parents, as I did at my son's IEP, wanted to see the whole menu.

At this juncture I was confused. I decided to do more research.

I have always said *if you want to understand what it's like to be deaf, you have to ask a deaf person.* So I flipped that on myself. It can also be said that *if you want to understand what it's like to have a cochlear implant, you have to ask a person who has a cochlear implant.*

I've asked around. I've heard incredible success stories. I've heard some horror stories. I've heard a lot of in-between stories. But I really wanted to get the facts straight from the kids.

I looked around again. I got wind of the 2011 Northeast Cochlear Implant Conference in Sturbridge, Massachussetts. They had a guest blogger, Jennifer Borhegyi, sharing updates of all the proceedings. I read the whole thing with much interest.

Another disclaimer: The vast majority of experiences shared were positive. The conference was a success. I'm aware of that. At the same time, to show we can't ignore the wide range of needs deaf and hard of hearing children have, I'm going to focus on one event. It was this one event that made me realize we should never take it for granted that any deaf kid is "doing just fine." Even the ones with cochlear implants.

I was intrigued by an event called *We Hear You, Now You Hear Us* featuring a panel of middle school and high school students who have cochlear implants.

When kids are given the green light to tell you what's going on and how they genuinely feel about it, they'll talk. And if we're smart enough, we'll listen.

The kids' comments were straightforward. They gave everyone a good look at their world. Among the things they said, as reported by the aforementioned guest blogger:

1. As with any kids, they're all into their cell phones and social media.

2. They make good use of the supports offered at their respective schools. This includes notetakers, Communication Access Realtime Translation (CART), C-Print, and preferential seating.

3. They enjoy music. They can connect their CI processors directly to an iPod. They can link a t-coil to earbuds, and so on. And while they do enjoy music, they say it also helps to be able to access the lyrics online (I can relate. Having access to lyrics helped me survive music class).

4. They participate in sports, but in that environment, they wind up asking their friends to repeat what the coaches said.

5. They enjoy movies as well, but noted that it's not worth going to a movie theater if there aren't any captions. They prefer to rent videos that have captions. *Note: Today, more and more movie theaters are showing open-captioned movies. I'm sure the kids from that panel, as well as countless other deaf and hard of hearing people, greatly appreciate this.*

6. Sleepovers, like sports, are also an environment where it's hard to keep up with what others are saying. A comment was made about being "the first to fall asleep, the last to wake up."

I take back what I said earlier. *Madness in the Mainstream* is not going to be obsolete anytime soon. Its truths apply to deaf and hard of hearing children of all backgrounds.

Bottom line: Push aside all of the fuss about sign language versus cochlear implants for a moment. Early language acquisition is important. We know that. But it's also important to be aware of issues behind the scenes. The message we're giving our kids. The opportunities we offer them.

Are we opening doors for them? Are we encouraging them to lead authentic lives? Of course, this is what we want. And it requires a level of awareness that goes beyond sign language and assistive devices. We have to put all the pieces together in a way that people with opposing viewpoints probably never will.

More often than not, you'll find yourself sorting through a lot of conflicting information. A lot of myths and misconceptions. We're going to take a good look at that next.

Mythbusters

Now for the fun part. Mythbusters. There are so many myths out there. There are myths that are so blatantly absurd, it's almost comical. Let's bust them.

Myth Number 1: You need to keep your deaf child separate from other deaf people.

Hard to believe, but this myth is still out there and people still believe it. We live in an age where schools celebrate Diversity Day, yet deaf kids with different backgrounds are often not allowed to interact with each other. Usually it's the kids who use sign language and those who don't (especially if they have cochlear implants). They're kept apart as if they're going to cross-contaminate each other or something.

It needs to be said that deaf children benefit immensely when they have the opportunity to meet other deaf people with different backgrounds. It helps them find their place in this world. It shows them there's more than one way to succeed. It instills confidence. If you see another deaf person succeeding with a different approach than yours, that's good information to have. It's *reassuring* information. It's reassuring because in the back of your mind, you'll know that if what you're doing doesn't work, you'll find something else that does.

I could go on forever about the value of role models. The best role model for a deaf person is another deaf person. It's a support system. I'm sorry, but if you're a mainstreamed deaf student, it doesn't matter what kind of supplementary aids and services you get; you're always going to be *That Deaf Kid.* You could be *That Deaf Kid with the Interpreter, That Deaf Kid with the Cochlear Implant,* or *That Deaf Kid with the Captioning Machine.* You're still *That Deaf Kid.* The best way to overcome this is to have access to other deaf kids. You're no longer *That Deaf Kid* when you have a healthy dose of interaction time with your actual peers.

Myth Number 2: Sign language will hurt your English.

No. Let me clarify: *Lack of language* will hurt your English. As mentioned earlier, the brain does not care how you acquire language. It just wants language, period. As early as possible. Brain food.

The deaf kids who are reading and writing below age-appropriate levels are the ones who were language-deprived during the most critical early years of their lives.

Remember the movie *Meet the Fockers?* Robert DeNiro played an obsessed grandfather hellbent on teaching sign language to his infant grandson. DeNiro was spot-on. Sign language offers a head start for early language acquisition. Babies can learn and use sign language long before their vocal cords are fully developed.

The irony is that while there are countless babies learning sign language worldwide, most of them are *hearing.* If the benefits are so obvious, and the research shows they are, why are we withholding this from the *deaf* kids who need it the most? The brain is starved for language. Again, brain food.

Myth Number 3: Deaf children with cochlear implants should not be exposed to sign language.

Keep in mind that the cochlear implant is not *perfect*. There will always be auditory information that falls through the cracks. Sign language can help close the gap. There's research validating this. Here's an example:

"Sign vocabulary acquired before cochlear implantation supports rather than impedes acquisition of spoken vocabulary, and the introduction of new words in sign as well as speech supports their acquisition in spoken form."

"Expressive use of signs supports, and is not detrimental to, children's use of speech when diagnosis and intervention occur early."

—Mark Marschark, Ph.D. & Patricia E. Spencer, Ph.D.

Evidence of Best Practice Models and Outcomes in the Education of Deaf and Hard of Hearing Children: An International Review (2009)

I don't have a cochlear implant so I can't speak for all of the people who have one. But I do have an experience I'd like to share with you that shows how sign language can close a gap.

In my early years, I was hard of hearing. It wouldn't be a stretch to say that I could hear as well as kids of a similar age who nowadays have cochlear implants.

When I was seven or eight years old, one of my best friends was a kid named Donny. He lived right down the street from me.

Donny was the youngest of four kids. He had three older sisters and got bossed around a lot. It was not uncommon for any of them to yell at him at the drop of a hat.

One day, I was with Donny in his backyard when the screen door bust open. One of his sisters admonished him for something and, as she always did, started by yelling *"what's your problem?"* It must have been her catchphrase because she said it all the time.

But I had a problem with the word *problem.* No matter how many times Donny's sister said it, I could not understand it. I could only understand two-thirds of her famous catchphrase:

"What's your blblm?"

This is because the sounds *p, b,* and *m* are just about impossible to lipread. They look identical.

If you tell me that Paul went to the mall to buy a ball, you're going to overload the circuits in my brain.

I scratched my head and shrugged as Donny's sister yelled at him for the eight thousand and forty-seventh time.

"What's your blblm?"

I had no idea what was going on.

A short time later, my parents took me to the deaf club with them.

Yes, my parents are deaf and they took me to deaf clubs. I saw a lot of interesting stuff going on. That's another subject for another book at another time.

I had no interest in the debauchery going on in the deaf club. I played hide and seek with a friend instead. I went downstairs to hide in the coat room, where I encountered two deaf women who were either gossiping or arguing. I'm not sure what the conversation was about, but I did catch this one phrase in ASL:

"What's your problem?"

I froze in my tracks. I recognized the words. I was shocked at how I understood the context of the whole phrase.

So I walked up and interrupted what was a heated discussion.

I think I defused it, too. Those two ladies went from angry expression to confused expression really quick.

"What's this word?" I asked. I repeated the sign that was used for the word *problem*.

"Problem," said one of the women.

"Can you fingerspell that?" I asked.

"P-R-O-B-L-E-M," she responded.

"Cool! Thank you!" I ran off with a broad grin, leaving behind two very confused people.

The next day I was back in Donny's backyard when once more, the screen door bust open.

"What's your problem?" his sister barked.

Holy crap! I heard it! The whole thing!

By "heard it," I mean I really, really heard it. Clear as day. *What's. Your. Problem.*

Know what happened there? When that bewildered lady signed and then fingerspelled the word *problem,* she effectively wired my brain to hear it. Which I soon did.

This is why many deaf kids, including those at the previously discussed cochlear implant conference, like to look up song lyrics online. We can program our brains to recognize the words. Sign language, as you just saw in that *What's Your Problem* fiasco, does exactly the same.

Last but not least, we can smash this myth by going back to that cochlear implant conference. One of the speakers, Dr. Amy Szarkowski, is a Psychologist in the Deaf and Hard of Hearing Program at Boston Children's Hospital and an Instructor in the Department of Psychiatry at Harvard Medical School. She shared some fascinating research about quality of life for deaf and hard of hearing children.

Among her findings:

1. Deaf children who are members of the deaf community have a quality of life that is similar to those in the general population.

2. Hard of hearing kids are often in limbo between two worlds. The struggle of not fitting in here and not fitting in there can result in identity and socialization issues. (In fact, this is the reason I published a book titled *On the Fence: The Hidden World of the Hard of Hearing.*)

3. Younger deaf kids with cochlear implants (ages 8-12) have a lower quality of life than their hearing counterparts.

4. For deaf kids with cochlear implants in the 13-16 age bracket, no difference was found when comparing their quality of life with hearing children of a similar age.

Now here's the kicker: Dr. Szarkowski also revealed that...

5. Deaf children who effectively use both cochlear implants *and* sign language to communicate with deaf and hearing people alike have the highest quality of life.

Dr. Szarkowski's findings answered a question I had in mind for a long time: *If cochlear implants are so wonderful, why do many deaf college students with cochlear implants choose to attend deaf programs such as Gallaudet University or the National Technical Institute for the Deaf?*

Of course, there are many other deaf college students who attend hearing universities, but still... one way or the other, later in life deaf people (including those with cochlear implants) tend to gravitate toward each other. It significantly improves quality of life when you meet people who are *just like you.* I just wish deaf kids had this opportunity at a much earlier age.

Myth Number 4: If you allow exposure to other deaf people, you could lose your child to deaf culture.

This is similar to Myth Number 1, where people think they have to separate this deaf kid from that deaf kid. Only this time the fear is that if you introduce deaf kids to the deaf community, *poof,* they're gone. They'll join some underground radical deaf culture group and you'll never hear from them again.

Let's have fun with this one, shall we?

I'm deaf. As is my wife. We are active members of the deaf community. We have raised *hearing children.* We send our hearing kids to hearing schools, and...

THEY KEEP COMING BACK!

We can't get rid of them. We wake them up, feed them, and at 7:00am we send them on their way to their respective hearing schools. At 3:00pm, *they're baaaaack!* No matter how many times we kick them out, they keep coming back!

We don't "lose" our hearing kids to the hearing community. They *gain* enriching experiences in their hearing schools with their hearing friends, and they come home with exciting stories to tell us. Nothing wrong with that.

Likewise, when our first child went deaf and it became obvious that mainstreaming was not the least restrictive environment for him, we sent him to a deaf school. Guess what happened? This kid, who was miserable in the mainstream, found his place in a deaf school. He was so happy there. Instead of coming home and mumbling school was *meh,* he would share stories about sports teams, social events, and more.

We didn't lose a deaf kid to anything. We *gained* a happier kid. They don't call it *Deaf Gain* for nothing. Enough said.

Stress Management

Early in my career as a school counselor, I had the honor of attending a conference featuring Dr. Sam Trychin. I'd heard about him before, but up until that point I'd never seen him in person.

Dr. Trychin is hard of hearing. That's something I once was, but no longer am. I figured this presentation would be nothing more than an entertaining walk down memory lane. I was sure that it wouldn't apply to me at all.

I was wrong.

Dr. Trychin gave a fascinating keynote address. He shared several anecdotes about the hard of hearing experience, including a few hilarious misunderstandings that had everyone chuckling. But as Dr. Trychin pointed out, it was not entirely a laughing matter.

Included in the daily grind of being hard of hearing are some not so funny physical and emotional symptoms. The mental stress of constantly trying to keep up with what people are saying can bring forth some very real problems such as muscle tension, fatigue, high blood pressure, anxiety, irritability, headaches, stomach disorders, and more.

As I soaked up all of this information, suddenly I recalled those dreaded days when I had to sit up front, read lips, wear my hearing aid, and still make a fool out of myself with misunderstandings galore.

"Holy smokes," I said to a friend sitting next to me. "I'm a recovering HOH!" We laughed, but didn't think much about it afterward.

And then, a few months later, I blew out my back lifting heavy furniture. To my relief, an MRI indicated it was not a severe injury. A follow-up evaluation with a physical therapist revealed unusual tightness in the muscles supporting my back. This, more than the heavy furniture, was what caused the trouble. It was like a tight rubber band just about ready to snap, an accident waiting to happen. The heavy furniture simply pushed it over the edge.

That's when I knew.

All those years of sit up front and read lips? It was both mentally AND physically exhausting. I had twisted myself into a pretzel.

It gets worse. A few months later, there was a team-building activity at work. We had to form a line and give each other backrubs.

That was awkward.

Of course, the person behind me was a physical therapist. She squeezed my traps and gasped.

"Your muscles are *tight*," she exclaimed.

"That's not from weightlifting," I replied. "That's from years of tension in the mainstream."

It's true. Being mainstreamed, especially if you're *That Deaf Kid*, is stressful on so many levels. I had scrunched my shoulders for so long, the surrounding muscles were hard as a rock.

There's more.

While surfing the Internet, I came across a blog called The Limping Chicken. There was an article by Ian Noon, titled The impact of concentration fatigue on deaf children should be factored in.

Noon went into great detail about how exhausting concentration fatigue can be. He disclosed how reading lips and having to be attentive all day long completely wiped him out. When he got home, he would collapse on the sofa.

"I'm not just tired," he wrote. "I'm shattered."

It's a lot of work when you have to process bits and pieces of stuff you didn't fully understand. You have to figure out context, fill in the blanks, and come up with a reasonably intelligent response if someone asks you a question. It's mentally draining.

"It's like doing jigsaws, Suduku and Scrabble all at the same time," Noon added.

Let's take this a step further.

What happens when you put a deaf kid in an environment where every day, he has to deal with a significant amount of stress and concentration fatigue?

"@#%&!!!!"

That's what happens. Pardon my French.

I can explain.

One morning as I got ready to leave for work, I noticed that Darren, my then-mainstreamed son, had yet to get out of bed. He normally got ready at about the same time I did, and he was nowhere to be seen.

I went into his room and saw what happened. He had inadvertently set his alarm clock for 6:00pm instead of 6:00am. He was still snoozing. Sawing a log. So I woke him up.

Can you believe what he said?

"@#%&!!!!"

The kid dropped an F-bomb on me.

Such language. I have no idea where he picked it up. Probably from his mother. But geez. What just happened? All I did was let him know it was time for school and...

"@#%&!!!!"

That's when the flashbacks hit. It wasn't his mom. It was me. Back in the day when I was mainstreamed, I would wake up every morning and say the same thing.

"@#%&!!!!"

That's two generations of F-bombs every morning. It's a hell of a family legacy.

Bonus news coverage: My daughter Lacey recently lost her hearing. As of this writing, she's still attending a mainstream school. It's tough. You might like to know she has shown us it's not just the guys in the family who are capable of some rather colorful language.

But seriously, is this what we want for our deaf and hard of hearing children? For them to *dread* going to school every day?

Conversely, I have worked in a deaf school for over twenty-five years. I eventually transferred Darren to one, and am glad I did. Guess what I noticed? In deaf schools, it's the opposite reaction. The kids dread *missing* school. They have serious FOMO.

I can't tell you how many times we've had a kid come to school sick and then he protests when we have to send him home.

"No! I like it here!"

That speaks volumes. We should strive to make every educational setting for deaf and hard of hearing children a place where they genuinely want to be.

It's Time for the Madness to Stop

There are several steps that can be taken to ensure that deaf and hard of hearing children can have the kind of accessible, rewarding experience that *least restrictive environment* intended for them.

Among them:

1. Include deaf professionals in the decision-making process. If you're being advised about educational placement, supplemental aids and services, medical intervention and so on, look around you. Are there any deaf professionals involved? If yes, great. If no, find them and get their input as well. This does not mean that the hearing people advising you have no idea what they're doing. It's simply due diligence. You have every right to see the full menu.

2. Role models, role models, role models. Cannot emphasize this enough. The best cure for being *That Deaf Kid* is to meet other deaf kids (as well as deaf adults who are successful in their careers, as this eliminates any self-imposed glass ceiling).

3. Be on top of, and advocate for, any legislation that supports the needs of deaf and hard of hearing children. For example, the Alice Cogswell and Anne Macy Sullivan Act. You can get involved and make a difference.

4. While a title such as *Madness in the Mainstream* makes it sound like every mainstream school is a living hell for deaf children, this is simply not true. There *are* mainstream schools

that have excellent programs for deaf and hard of hearing children. We need the mainstream programs that do get it to share their expertise with the ones that don't. Most important, we need to push for these mainstream schools with deaf children to include *multiple* deaf children, and allow them ample opportunities to interact with each other.

5. Collaboration is needed between deaf schools and mainstream schools. Deaf schools should be encouraged to establish satellite programs where their staff (and students) can become valuable resources for mainstream schools. There's one deaf school, for example, that has an afterschool program where mainstreamed deaf kids can join the residential students for evening study hall and social events. This kind of arrangement is a win-win for everyone.

6. Summer camps / weekend programs for deaf and hard of hearing children. These are valuable learning and socialization experiences, especially for mainstreamed deaf and hard of hearing students who might not otherwise have the opportunity to meet and interact with their deaf peers. There are several traditional deaf camps (such as Camp Mark Seven in Old Forge, New York), or you could go with educational camps such as summer programs offered by Gallaudet University and the National Technical Institute for the Deaf. There are sports camps as well. Search for them, and you'll find them. You'll be glad you did.

That Deaf Kid Will Be All Right

There's no greater relief for *That Deaf Kid* than finding out he or she is not *The Only One*. This applies to everybody, really. It even applies to my hearing son, Brandon, who attended a summer camp for CODAs (Children of Deaf Adults). Brandon was thrilled to find out he was not *The Only One* who had a, shall we say, interesting family dynamic going on.

Then there's Lacey, whose life was flipped when she went from CODA to *That Deaf Kid* practically overnight. Late deafness is no joke. It's been a roller coaster. But just the same, it helps Lacey, and many others, to know she's not *The Only One*.

Which brings us full circle to Darren, the original *That Deaf Kid* who inspired *Madness in the Mainstream*. Although his journey was as much of a roller coaster as anyone else's, there was something we did for him in the early going to let him know he was not *The Only One*.

Darren's elementary school provided him with just about all of the supplementary aids and services we requested. And you'd think that hey, having deaf parents would give him a strong dose of a healthy deaf identity.

But it's more complicated than that. He was still surrounded by hearing teachers and hearing classmates. It's only natural he wanted to emulate them as best as he could. The *it's a hearing world* introject is a tough one to beat.

So what did we do? We took Darren on a visit to the Pennsylvania School for the Deaf to watch the boys varsity basketball team play against the New York School for the Deaf. It was a packed gym full of deaf athletes and spectators.

For the first time in a long time, Darren got to see *deaf* as *normal* on a much larger scale. (My home doesn't qualify as *normal*, as many friends will attest.)

Darren not only enjoyed the game, but he also gleefully pointed out that he could understand everything the coaches and players said on the sidelines.

At halftime, Darren was on cloud nine as some of the players walking toward the locker room stopped to say hello and shake hands with him.

Yes, I know this is just high school basketball. But to an eight-year-old kid, it was like meeting LeBron James.

And then Carl Way, a teacher aide at PSD, approached us. Carl had known Darren since he was a baby. But what he didn't know was that Darren had recently gone deaf. Carl was taken by surprise when he noticed a hearing aid on Darren's ear.

"You're deaf?" Carl asked.

Darren nodded yes.

Carl broke into a huge smile.

You had to know Carl to know that his smile lit up a room like no other. It had magical powers.

"You-me... SAME!" Carl signed in ASL. He laughed and gave Darren a high five.

You should have seen the smile on Darren's face.

It was at that moment when I knew *That Deaf Kid* would be all right.

BONUS MATERIAL

The following section has been added to this book as a bonus. Everything prior is an almost verbatim collection of material from my *Madness in the Mainstream* presentation. Everything in this bonus section came from follow-up questions, recommendations, or some spontaneous inspiration that's somehow connected to all of this.

When you're a guest speaker, you inevitably meet people who ask really good questions. I've met plenty. This includes an eighth-grade student who absolutely *stumped* me. I was only able to give him a guesstimate for an answer.

Of course, the correct answer popped up at 4:00am the next day. It's a powerful answer and I've added it here. I hope that kid reads it. I'm grateful that he kick-started my mind the way he did.

Another guest speaking gig involved a class at West Chester University. The teacher, an old colleague of mine, had every student in his class prepare at least two questions in advance. The questions were *deep*. They infused my mind with new ideas. You'll find some of them here.

Then there was an encore at the University of Pennsylvania. A few years after my original presentation, they invited me back... for eight minutes.

That's right. Eight minutes. It was as part of a larger panel and each of us was allotted eight minutes to say what we had to say. And then they opened the floor for a question and answer session that went on for over an hour. Again, great questions. Again, mind blown.

Questions are good. Especially when it comes to issues related to the deaf and hard of hearing. As you've already read, we're experts at social bluffing. But if you ask a genuine question... you'll get a genuine answer.

These bonus chapters are inspired by some of the best questions I've ever been asked.

Enjoy.

The Stumper

During a guest speaking session with students at Germantown Friends School, an eighth-grade student asked me a mind-boggling question.

"If you lost your hearing at age five and didn't have a sign language interpreter in school until you were fifteen, how did you pick up language in between? Shouldn't you have been stuck at the level of a five-year-old?"

Awesome question!

I didn't know how to answer it.

My only answer for this bright young man was "Reading. Lots and lots of reading."

Well, yes, to some extent that's true. I was a bookworm. I would sit cluelessly in a class full of hearing students I could not understand, and then I would ask someone for that day's homework assignment. Afterward, I'd run to the library and catch up on whatever I missed.

So it was my reading ability, I surmised, that saved the day.

Wrong.

Reading was only part of the equation. Where do you think I got the ability to pull off such a feat in the first place?

That's right. Early language acquisition. Between birth and age five, my parents had signed to me. My brain was thus effectively "wired" for language. This is what allowed me to continue to expand my vocabulary through the years in spite of the obstacles my hearing loss and educational placement had presented.

I've already dedicated a lot of my writing and presentation material to the topic of social bluffing. My reason for blowing it out of the water is to raise awareness in such a manner that deaf and hard of hearing children no longer feel an obligation to do this.

Your school years are not the time and place to practice social bluffing. It's the time and place to learn. And the foundation for that is pretty much set between the ages of zero and five. At that age, your brain is like a huge sponge. It's ready to absorb as much information as possible.

At my age, your brain is like a hockey puck. We really need to take advantage of that sponge in the early going.

In my book *On the Fence: The Hidden World of the Hard of Hearing,* there's a fascinating article by Jerel Barnhart, Ph.D. He explains the concept of plasticity and its application to language acquisition for deaf and hard of hearing children. Here's an excerpt:

Regarding research in learning of language, there are extensive studies that indicate the "plasticity" of newborns' brains. That is, they are able to learn and develop neural pathways quickly and easily. As a child ages, there is less plasticity and less chance of establishing neural pathways in learning new information such as language. There are indications that as early as age three, children begin losing that plasticity. By age five, it is considered that a child who hasn't been exposed to language will probably always be at a disadvantage at learning language and other verbal processes such as spelling and writing.

Now *this* is what effectively answers that eighth-grader's fascinating question. Without a doubt, it was my exposure to language between birth and age five that laid the groundwork for everything else.

Ironically, our awareness of plasticity also fuels the increasing number of cochlear implant surgeries for infants and toddlers. The irony doesn't escape me that plasticity applies to *both* cochlear implants and sign language, and yet we have so many people separating them in an endless either/or argument.

Nonetheless, Dr. Barnhart, who is deaf and has a cochlear implant himself, advocates on behalf of sign language for young children with cochlear implants. His explanation is that infants can't sufficiently "work" with their audiologists during the mapping sessions that enhances their ability to use their cochlear implants. An older child or adult can provide accurate feedback to an audiologist, but an infant cannot.

There is also the matter of how much a child can hear versus how much a child *understands.* This is why Dr. Barnhart strongly recommends the use of sign language for all children, including those with cochlear implants, in order to "provide the best opportunity for a child to learn language at an early age."

It doesn't have to be either/or. If you prefer a hearing aid or a cochlear implant, that's fine. At the same time, sign language does not have to be excluded. Sign language is truly a gift.

For everyone, deaf and hearing alike.

A Finely Cut Diamond

Someone asked me why I support the use of sign language when "99.9% of the world uses speech."

I don't know what the actual percentage is. But just for the sake of argument, let's assume this guy had his numbers right. I'll play along.

I've said it before and I'll say it again: It wasn't until I discovered peers and role models in the deaf community when I learned how to really connect with people on a different level. Conversations suddenly became deeper and more meaningful.

These conversations were (and still are) in sign language. It's one hundred percent accessible. There's none of the fill-in-the-blanks guesswork that comes with lipreading.

Years ago, when a group of hearing friends burst out in laughter, I would either ignore it and smile along like an idiot, or ask a trusted friend to repeat what was said. He would usually comply, but it was not the same. I was playing catch-up. The moment itself was gone. Or, as the notoriously famous deaf quote goes, *train gone.*

You simply can't take those magic, spontaneous moments and recreate them. It just doesn't work when you say, "Hold it, everyone say that all over again for the deaf guy."

There's a natural flow to deep, intimate conversations. They just happen, and you're either fully involved in the moment or you're not. It's a spiritual aspect of our lives that is often overlooked but essential to all of us.

There's nothing wrong with deaf people connecting with the hearing world through whatever means are available. Nothing wrong with doing our part to meet hearing people halfway. It could be with speech, pen and paper, gesturing, interpreters, text messages, and so on (and if we happen to meet hearing people who know sign language, that's a much-appreciated bonus). Bottom line: whatever works, we'll do our part.

But the fact of the matter is, it's still that .1% which allows many of us to learn about ourselves and connect with others on a much deeper level. Certainly, the larger 99.9% is a huge rock that dwarfs the remaining .1%. But it's bigger only in terms of size.

If your child has a lot in common with people in that little .1%, it is absolutely worth seeking out. It might be dwarfed by the other 99.9%, but that little .1% is a rare, finely cut diamond that has all the value and beauty in the world.

The Best-Kept Secret

I once had the honor of doing a keynote presentation at a National Counselors of the Deaf Association conference. It was the first time in a while that I had presented to a predominantly deaf audience.

The presentation focused on how deaf mainstreamed students fly under the radar at their respective programs, doing well academically but struggling in other key areas that teachers and administrators might overlook.

Mainstreamed deaf students put in a lot of effort to succeed. They have a vast array of survival skills that help them get through the day. But no matter how well they pull this off, they still have to deal with gaps in incidental learning, meaningful relationships, and self-esteem. There's also the stigma that comes with being *That Deaf Kid* if you happen to be the only deaf person in your school.

Most mainstreamed deaf students willingly go through this. Based on perceived attitudes from teachers, classmates, families, and medical professionals, they internalize the belief that it's entirely their responsibility to assimilate into the Hearing World. Sometimes, when it gets too frustrating, they'll fake it. They'll utilize clever strategies such as social bluffing.

This takes an incredible amount of hard work. And many of these kids don't realize how hard they're working because they don't have a frame of reference. They've never had the opportunity to be in a classroom with other deaf kids.

At just about all of my presentations, audiences are surprised when they find out how the misinterpretation of *least restrictive environment* has created so many problems.

There's a reason I say LRE stands for legislators ruined everything.

But with a deaf audience at the NCDA conference, I was besieged with an entirely different reaction.

"OH... MY... GOD. I went through exactly the same thing."

The deaf professionals in the audience knew precisely where I was coming from. They had *lived* it.

Why don't more people in mainstream society seek out the services of deaf professionals, deaf role models, and deaf mentors? They are the best-kept secret for parents of deaf children. If you really want to know what it's like to be deaf, ask a deaf person. There's so much we can share with you.

Unfortunately, the vast majority of parents who have deaf children don't get the opportunity to connect with the deaf community. Instead, they encounter medical professionals who focus primarily on auditory-verbal training. That's their job. But it needs to be pointed out that auditory-verbal training is just one aspect of the Whole Deaf Child.

Yes, there's more to it than that. Lots more.

Soon after the NCDA conference, I came across a powerful video by Rikki Poynter. She was twenty-four years old at the time. She discussed in depth how she only recently came to terms with her deaf identity.

The video hit me to the core. My reaction?

OH... MY... GOD. I went through exactly the same thing.

Rikki's experience at age twenty-four is uncannily similar to my experience at age twenty-three. Which begs the question:

Why do we have to wait so long to find ourselves?

When you take an entirely pathological approach to deafness, the goal is fixing the ears. I get that. But this approach comes with a price. As I said in my presentation:

Their minds are so full of who they want us to be, they don't see who we really are.

If you want to empower deaf children to reach their fullest potential, the quickest path is to connect them with other deaf people. Deaf people from all walks of life. It's as simple as that.

We have gone through what your child is going through now. If you give us the opportunity to share our knowledge and expertise, it becomes easier for the next generation of deaf kids to navigate through life's inevitable roadblocks.

Awareness is the first step toward positive change. There are so many deaf people working hard to create this awareness.

They're trailblazers. Reach out to them, and you'll unlock the authentic self in your deaf child.

Rogue Role Model

In 1975, I lived in a small apartment with my parents in Mt. Airy, Philadelphia. There was no captioned TV, no videophones, no relay services, no text messaging... nothing.

Eventually, we got one of those noisy, mailbox-sized teletypewriters. We were then able to call other deaf family and friends. This was the start of a technological revolution that led to much-improved accessibility for the deaf.

Prior to these technological advances, getting in touch with people was a total crapshoot. When we had visitors, they often dropped by unannounced. They just drove over hoping that someone was home, and that they didn't drive all those miles for nothing.

One of these unannounced visitors was Joe, a childhood buddy of my dad's. I was nine years old at the time Joe stopped by, and it was the first time I'd ever seen him. He bear-hugged my dad and the two of them talked about the good old days over a few beers.

It wasn't long before Joe noticed that I was not quite deaf and not quite hearing. He was right. Back then, I was still hard of hearing. Doctors described it as a progressive sensorineural hearing loss. I took my time with the *progressive* part. It would take a few more years before my audiogram indicated I was profoundly deaf.

While my dad confirmed Joe's observation, he remarked that I had to wear two hearing aids at school and that I didn't like it.

Didn't like it? I hated it.

I hated wearing two hearing aids because my left ear and my right ear had totally different perceptions of sound. My left ear was more sensitive to sound—I could hear more things with it—while my right ear, although technically deafer, could *understand* more sounds. Back in those days, I could actually talk to people on the phone, so long as I held the phone up to my right ear. If I switched the phone to my left ear, their voices would become louder, but I could not understand a word they said.

For me, my comfort zone was to wear a hearing aid in my right ear while leaving my left ear alone. A hearing aid in my left ear was disorienting and gave me a headache. At school, I would turn the left hearing aid off and leave it that way—until the teacher did a hearing aid check and made me turn it back on. As soon as I got home, both hearing aids came off. I only used a hearing aid on my right ear when speaking on the phone, and eventually I stopped doing that after my parents got me a phone with a built-in amplifier.

After my dad explained all of this, Joe got up and walked toward me.

"Hey, Mark. Do you wear two hearing aids?" he asked.

"Yes."

"Do you like wearing two hearing aids?"

"No."

"Why not?"

"It gives me a headache."

"You prefer one hearing aid?"

"Yes. Just for my right ear."

"Then why wear two?"

"Because my teacher said so."

Joe knelt down so that he was at eye level with me.

"You tell your teacher that I said..."

Joe launched into a profanity-filled tirade.

"JOE!" my mom interrupted. She was shocked to see a grown man cussing in front of a nine-year-old.

I was shocked, too. For an entirely different reason.

For the first time in my life, I had a deaf guy telling me that hearing people can be wrong. It shook the foundation of the *follow-everything-the-hearing-folks-tell-me-to-do* world that I lived in.

"Hold on a second," Joe assured my mom. "I'm almost finished." He turned back to me and picked up where he left off.

"If you're not comfortable with two hearing aids, don't wear two hearing aids. If you want just one, wear one. If you want none, wear none. If you want three, what the hell, wear three."

Never mind that it's anatomically impossible to wear three hearing aids. This guy had my undivided attention.

"Don't let your teacher decide for you," Joe continued. "You're deaf. Don't let someone else tell you how to be deaf. Only you can be deaf the best way you can be deaf."

Joe shook my hand and I stood there in *awe*. This guy rocked. Who cares if my mom was mortified. Everything this guy said rang true.

At that point in my life, all of the decisions that were made for me were made by hearing people who not only insisted they knew what was best, but also overruled my deaf parents in the process. The message I internalized from this was *listen to all of the doctors, teachers, and audiologists. They are superior to your deaf family and the deaf community. Do what they say, no questions asked.*

And here we had a deaf guy telling me I didn't have to listen to all of these people. For the first time, I felt validated. Joe and I had the same feelings about the world around us. It was genuine. For the others, the people for whom I reluctantly wore two hearing aids, it was a stressful relationship.

I smiled when Joe bid farewell after his visit. And then I never saw him again.

The following week, I was back in my classroom, wearing one hearing aid. It was a small victory. Unfortunately, since I was the only deaf student in the whole school, the lack of support and the isolation of the mainstream caused me to go back to my old ways. I returned to the *follow-everything-the-hearing-folks-tell-me-to-do* world that inwardly made my stomach churn. I rarely vented my frustration about it. And, even more sadly, Joe and his powerful words faded away.

It would take another thirteen years—when the Deaf President Now protest went on at Gallaudet University in 1988—before I realized once again that deaf people can, and should, speak up.

Role models are priceless. Even the ones who cuss at nine-year-olds.

That Dad and That Tree

In the sports world, everyone knows about *That Dad*. The one who interrupts the ball game to give his kid unsolicited advice. The one who annoys the players, coaches, and umpires alike. Not to mention his own kid.

During the ride home, *That Dad* wants to do a play-by-play analysis of a game that ended a long time ago. His kid, on the other hand, would be more interested in stopping somewhere for ice cream.

I've used *That Dad* to make a critical point about assistive technology for deaf and hard of hearing children. There is nothing inherently wrong with any assistive device that offers any number of benefits.

A deaf kid should be able to nonchalantly put on a hearing aid the same way people nonchalantly put their glasses on. If it helps, great. No need to make a big fuss over it.

But when a hearing aid or cochlear implant is *overemphasized* by a well-meaning parent or teacher, it changes the dynamic. Whether we realize it or not, we may be reinforcing an introject that's hard to shake:

You need to act hearing. It is your responsibility to assimilate.

I've talked about introjects for years. But just before a guest appearance at the University of Pennsylvania, someone brought it to my attention that there's another resource out there that drives the same point home in a different yet equally powerful way.

The resource? A book titled *Far From the Tree: Parents, Children, and the Search for Identity* by Andrew Solomon.

It's an eye-opener. Solomon goes into great detail about vertical and horizontal identities.

Vertical identities can be described as traits and identities that are inherited. They're passed *down* to you by your parents on the family tree.

If your parents are Irish, you're probably Irish, too. You didn't have much say in the matter.

Vertical identities don't have to be genetic. The language your family speaks and the religion they practice? Also passed down. Although you can go off in a different direction there. Which brings us to our next point:

No one is *exactly* like their parents. We have horizontal identities, too. Our horizontal identities move away from the family tree, in a direction our parents may not have anticipated or approved.

If you're deaf and your family is hearing, then you've strayed far from the tree.

I'm not going to do an in-depth analysis of vertical and horizontal identities. Solomon did an excellent job of that himself.

One thing I will do is highly recommend the book. Normally, I insist that *if you want to understand anything deaf-related, ask a deaf person.* Solomon is one of those rare people for whom I will make an exception.

Solomon immersed himself into the deaf world. Not to fix us. To understand us. His original intent was to write an article about deaf culture for *The New York Times.*

What started out as curiosity soon turned into fascination. He joined our world and came out of it with the inspiration for *Far From the Tree.*

I can respect that.

In the chapter on deafness as a horizontal identity, Solomon hit the nail on the head in such an insightful way that I personally brought his book to every presentation I did afterward.

That book is 962 pages. It took up a lot of space in my briefcase, but it was worth it.

There's something in there about the overemphasis of auditory-verbal therapy.

Sound familiar?

When AVT is overemphasized, as Solomon explains it, it "becomes that relationship." And a strained one at that. Just like the little leaguer and *That Dad.*

We live in a world that struggles to accept horizontal identities. Parents, either because of their own beliefs or beliefs imposed on them by society, may have a hard time accepting horizontal identities.

When it comes to deaf and hard of hearing children, parents often find themselves in an ongoing tug of war between AVT and sign language. They're usually told to choose one over the other.

Solomon, on the other hand, takes a different approach in *Far From the Tree.*

I can't possibly summarize the entire book in here. But here's what I did say during my eight minutes of fame at the University of Pennsylvania:

"See this book? *Far From the Tree.* I read it during my lunch break."

You could tell who in the audience already read the book. There were so many knowing glances.

"The author did a great job of explaining vertical and horizontal identities," I continued. "It's a lot to absorb."

I held up the book and flipped through the pages for emphasis.

"962 pages," I grinned.

"And nowhere in this book did I ever see Solomon say *choose one.*"

Horizontal identities can, and should, be embraced. The same goes for *That Deaf Kid.*

In my first book, *Deaf Again,* I started off with a powerful quote by E.E. Cummings. It sums up the experience of just about every deaf and hard of hearing student in the mainstream. I'd like to bring things full circle and close this book with the same quote:

The hardest fight a man has to fight is to live in a world where every single day someone is trying to make you someone you do not want to be.

Embrace who you are. All of it.

About the Author

Mark Drolsbaugh is the author of *Deaf Again*, *Anything But Silent*, and *Madness in the Mainstream*. He also collaborated with a team of other writers to publish *On the Fence: The Hidden World of the Hard of Hearing*. Mark lives in Lansdale, PA, with his wife Melanie and their three children. With a history of late deafness in his family, Mark has a unique perspective of what it's like to be hearing, hard of hearing, and deaf.

Read more at https://www.handwavepublications.com.